DINNER DECONSTRUCTED

ANNABEL STAFF

PAVILION

WELCOME TO
DINNER
DECONSTRUCTED!

Inside this book you will find 35 recipes, but this is not a traditional recipe book. In the following pages, you will see each recipe broken down into its main ingredients, then beautifully styled and photographed. It's up to you to guess what the recipe is! But don't worry, you'll find the answers at the back of the book, along with an easy-to-follow method for making each dish.

Why make such an unusual recipe book? Well, it turned out that people enjoyed the process of guessing what the recipe was from looking at the photos and would often stop me before I could tell them the 'answer'. This sparked the idea to move away from an already untraditional recipe book, into something more, a recipe quiz book if you like. Seeing how excited my friends were to work out the recipe and guess correctly really showed how much more potential there was than I had already imagined!

I hope you enjoy guessing the recipes as much as I loved making this book – enjoy!

#1

OLIVE OIL
GARLIC **ONION**
RED PEPPER SALT
PAPRIKA CUMIN
TOMATOES
CHILLI EGGS
PEPPER
PITTA **FETA**

#2

LEMON JUICE
AVOCADO **EGG**
OLIVE OIL SALT
BIRD'S-EYE CHILLI
SOURDOUGH
RADISH PEPPER

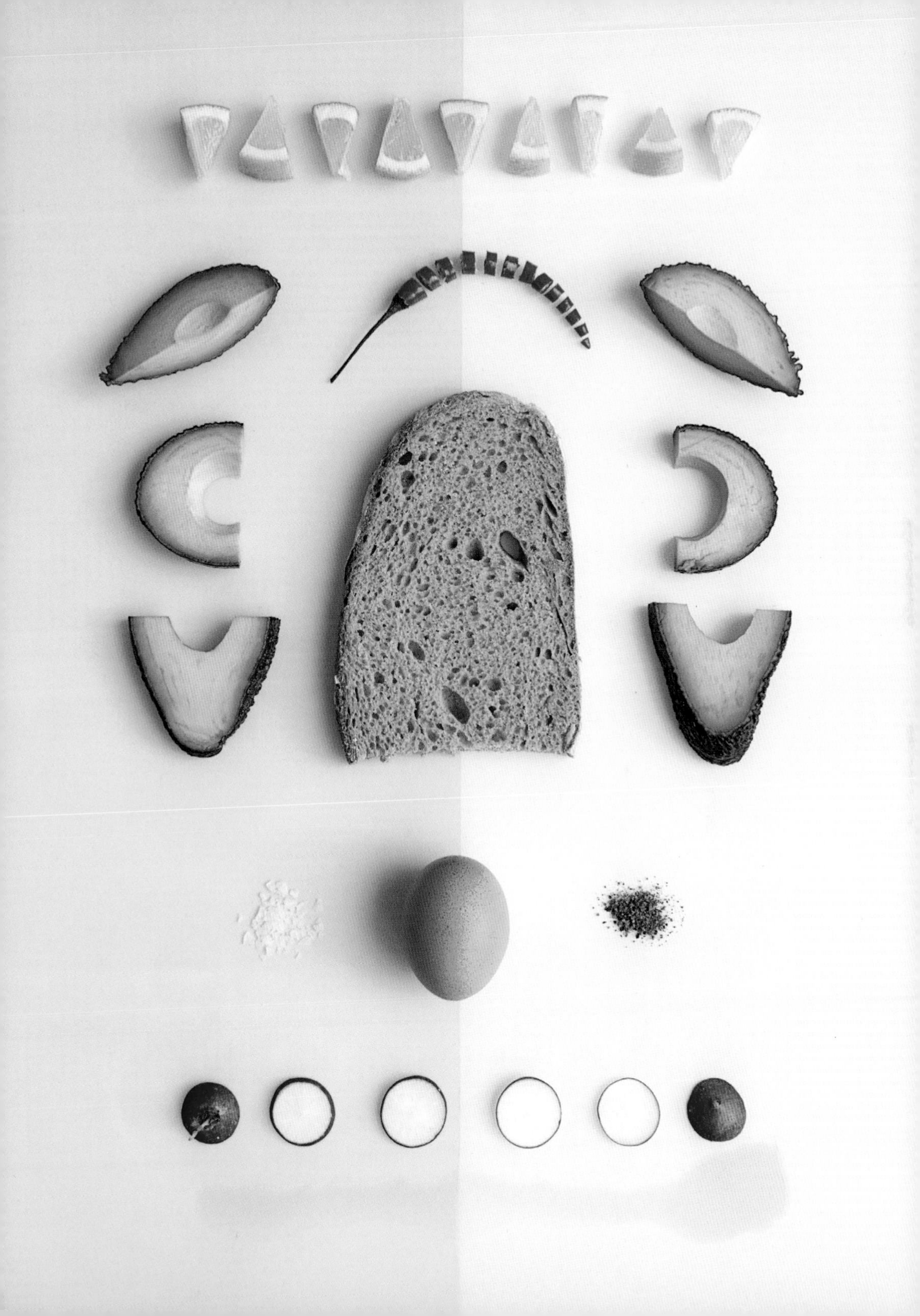

WHITE WINE VINEGAR
PEPPER BABY SPINACH
EGGS OLIVE OIL
PARMA HAM
ENGLISH MUFFIN
LEMON **DIJON**
JUICE **MUSTARD**
BUTTER SALT

#4

BASIL **EGGS**

SALT BUTTER

PEPPER

ONION BLUE
CHEESE

ASPARAGUS

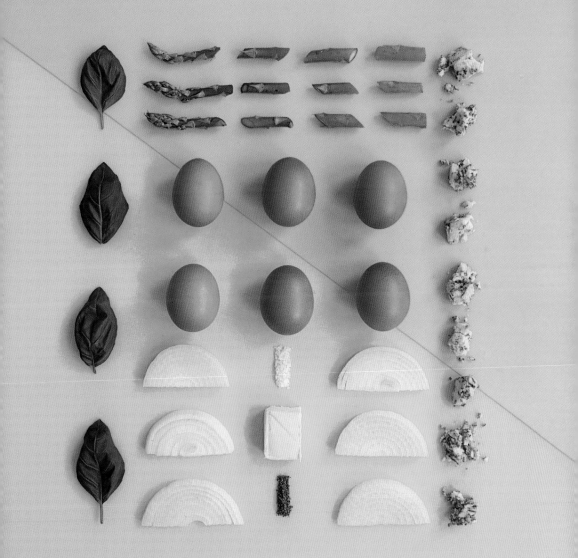

#5

MILK FLOUR
EGG **VANILLA**
BAKING POWDER
OIL **YOGURT**
SALT SUGAR
BLUEBERRIES

#6

MOZZARELLA
GARLIC BASIL
TOMATO **OLIVE**
PURÉE SALT **OIL**
CHERRY TOMATOES
MUSHROOMS
OLIVES PEPPER
CIABATTA **ROCKET**

MUSTARD
MINCED BEEF
BLUE CHEESE
RED ONION TOMATO
BURGER BUNS
CHILLI KETCHUP
SAUCE SALT PEPPER OIL
EGG GARLIC
ICEBERG LETTUCE

#8

MACARONI
CHEESE BUTTER
PEPPER MILK OIL
MUSTARD
PAPRIKA FLOUR
GARLIC SALT

#9

MINCED BEEF
KIDNEY PAPRIKA
BEANS CINNAMON
CUMIN PEPPER ONION
TOMATO PURÉE
CELERY GREEN
DRIED OREGANO PEPPER
GARLIC SALT
TOMATOES STOCK
OLIVE OIL CUBE
CHILLI POWDER

#10

CHICKEN BASIL
COCONUT MILK OIL
KAFFIR LIME LEAVES
FISH SAUCE GARLIC
THAI GREEN BROWN
CURRY PASTE SUGAR
PEPPER
SALT FINE GREEN BEANS

#11

MIXED HERBS TOMATOES
MINCED BEEF GARLIC
BROWN SUGAR
ONION PARMESAN
MOZZARELLA
LASAGNE TOMATO
OLIVE OIL **PEPPER** SALT PURÉE
BEEF STOCK CUBE

#12

TOMATOES PARMESAN
EGGS PEPPER
SALT
MOZZARELLA
CHILLI GARLIC
BREADCRUMBS BASIL
OLIVE OIL OREGANO
AUBERGINES
WATER ONION

#13

SALT **BAY LEAF** THYME
SPAGHETTI

OLIVE OIL

CARROTS

CELERY GARLIC

ONION PEPPER

STOCK CHICKEN

VEGETABLE OIL

#14

SWEETCORN
RED PEPPER STOCK
CHIVES PEPPER ONION
SALT MILK CELERY
FLOUR POTATO
OLIVE OIL GARLIC

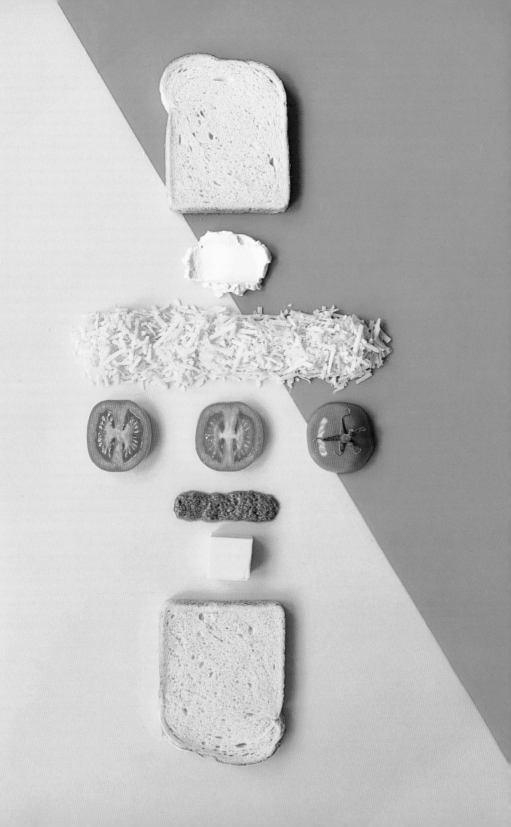

CHEDDAR PESTO
CREAM CHEESE BREAD
BUTTER TOMATO

#16

CAULIFLOWER

SPRING ONIONS BUTTER

BROCCOLI PAPRIKA

FLOUR CHEESE

MILK PEPPER SALT

MUSTARD

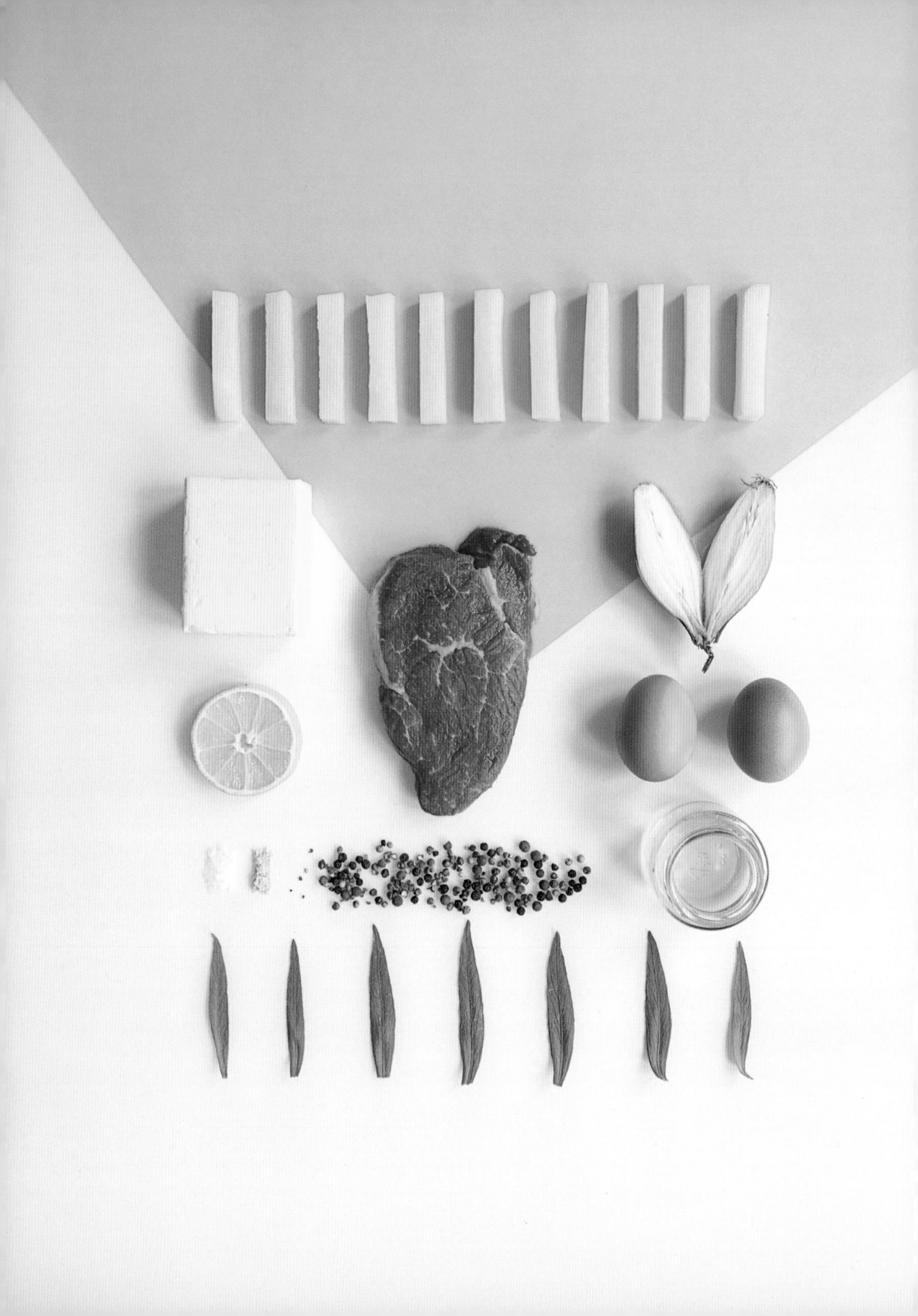

WHITE WINE VINEGAR
SHALLOT MUSTARD
TARRAGON SALT
RUMP STEAK
LEMON OLIVE OIL PEPPER
JUICE BUTTER EGGS
POTATOES OIL
PEPPERCORNS

#18

BUTTER SALT
BAY LEAF GARLIC
ONIONS STOCK
FLOUR THYME
GRUYÈRE **WINE** PEPPER
BAGUETTE

TUNA BASIL
SOURDOUGH **PEPPER**
SALT SPRING ONIONS
CHEDDAR PAPRIKA
MAYONNAISE

#20

GOLDEN SYRUP OATS
APRICOTS
BUTTER CHERRIES
MUSCOVADO SUGAR

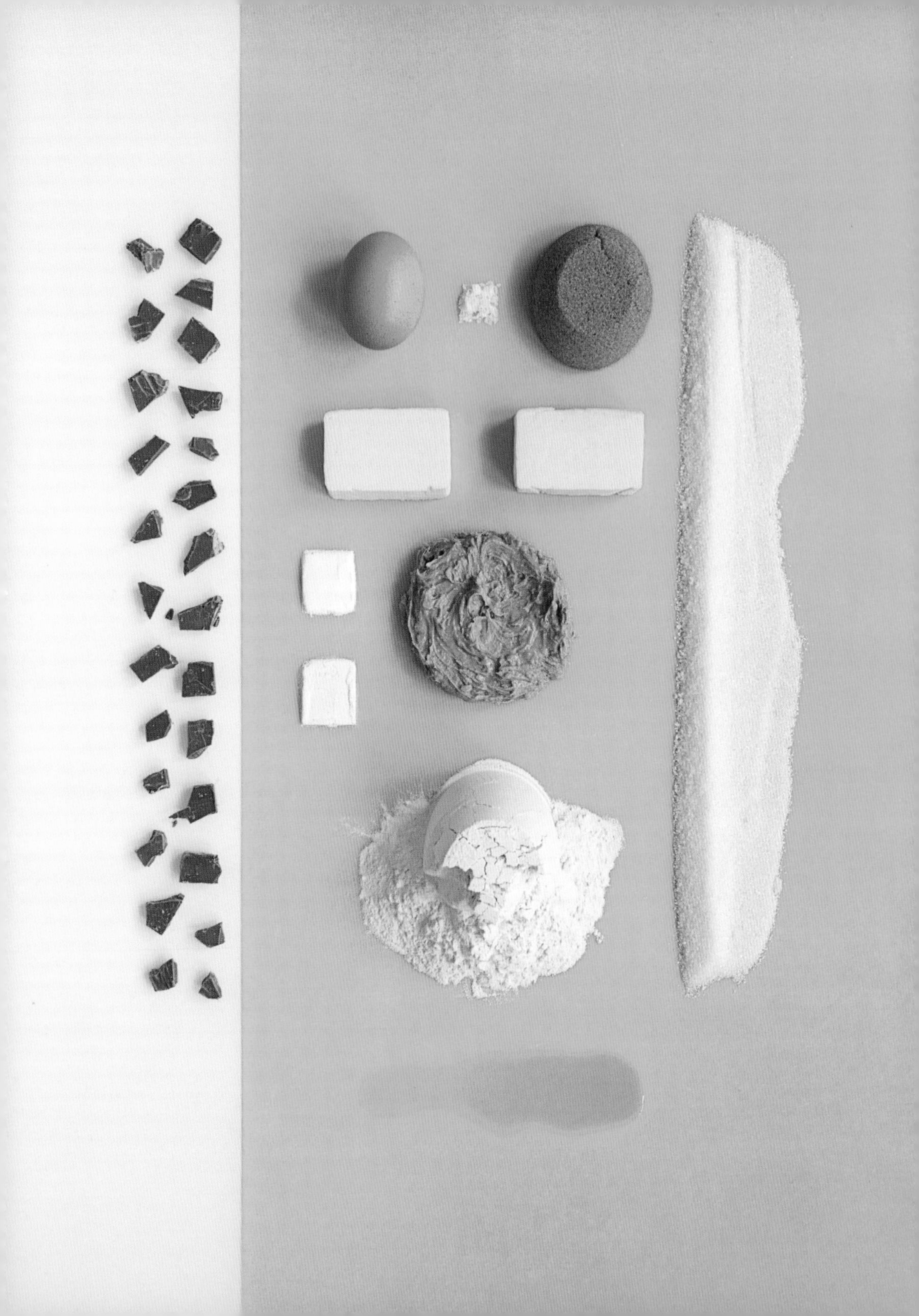

VANILLA BUTTER
BICARBONATE OF SODA
BAKING POWDER
PEANUT BUTTER SUGAR
EGG SALT FLOUR
CHOCOLATE CHIPS

#22

ROSEMARY WALNUTS
GARLIC CRANBERRIES
OLIVE OIL
CAMEMBERT
BAGUETTE

MILK OIL EGGS
SALT PEPPER THYME
MUSTARD FLOUR
SAUSAGES

#24

POTATOES CREAM
THYME NUTMEG
SALT MILK PEPPER
GARLIC PARMESAN

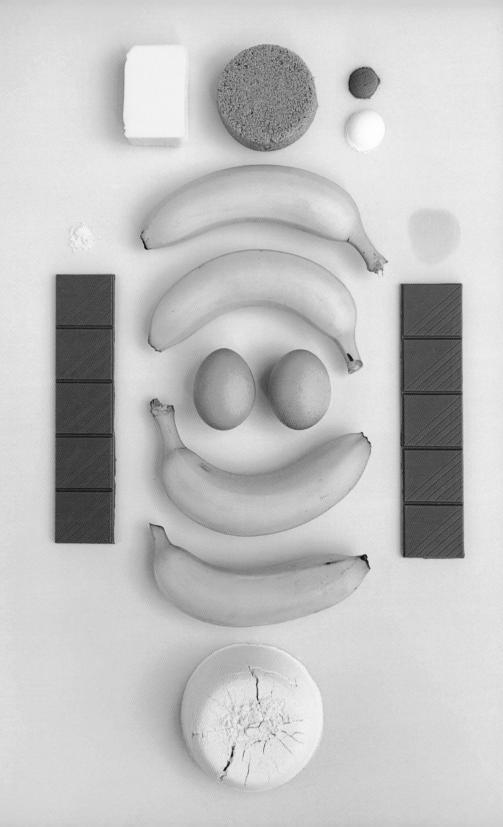

BANANAS EGGS
BICARBONATE OF SODA
FLOUR BROWN SUGAR
BUTTER VANILLA
CHOCOLATE SALT
CINNAMON

#26

OIL FLOUR VANILLA
BAKING CINNAMON
POWDER ICING SUGAR
SALT EGGS
BICARBONATE OF SODA SUGAR
WALNUTS CARROTS
CREAM
CHEESE BUTTER

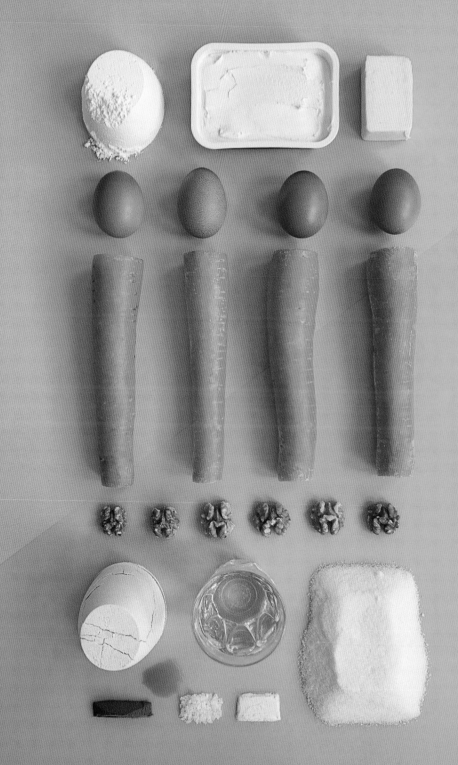

ICING SUGAR
PEANUT **VANILLA**
BUTTER BREAD
BANANA BUTTER
EGG CINNAMON

#28

BUTTER **OATS**
SUGAR CINNAMON
BLACKBERRIES
APPLES **FLOUR**

#29

AVOCADOS
CORIANDER JALEPEÑOS
LIME TOMATOES
TORTILLA CHIPS
GARLIC PEPPER
REFRIED BEANS
ONION CHEDDAR
SALT RED ONION

#30

GINGERNUTS
LIMES ICING SUGAR
EGG YOLKS
BUTTER CREAM
CONDENSED MILK

MOZZARELLA
GARLIC PARSLEY
BUTTER
BAGUETTE

#32

FETA CAYENNE

LIME PEPPER

CORN ON SALT
THE COB

MAYONNAISE

SOUR CREAM
OIL SALT CHILLI
RED PEPPER GARLIC
CHEDDAR PAPRIKA
CORIANDER TORTILLAS
PEPPER RED ONIONS
KIDNEY BEANS CUMIN

#34

MERINGUES
CREAM MINT
STRAWBERRIES

#35

CHICKPEAS
LEMON GARLIC
CUMIN TAHINI
PITTA
PAPRIKA SALT
OLIVE OIL

#1
SHAKSHUKA

1 TBSP OLIVE OIL
4 GARLIC CLOVES, CHOPPED
1 ONION, CHOPPED
1 RED (BELL) PEPPER, DICED
1 TSP PAPRIKA
1 TSP GROUND CUMIN
1 RED CHILLI, DESEEDED AND FINELY
  CHOPPED
SALT AND FRESHLY GROUND BLACK PEPPER
400 G/14 OZ CAN PLUM TOMATOES
75 G/2¾ OZ/⅔ CUP FETA CHEESE,
  CRUMBLED
4 EGGS
WARM PITTA BREAD, TO SERVE

Heat the oil in a deep frying pan over a medium heat. Stir in the garlic, onion and red pepper and sauté for about 5 minutes, or until the onion is soft.

Add the paprika, cumin and chilli and season to taste. Stir in the tomatoes and use the back of a spoon to break them up. Simmer for about 20 minutes, then stir in the crumbled feta.

Carefully crack the eggs into the tomato sauce. Cover and cook for 5 minutes, or until the egg whites are firm. If the tomato sauce gets dry, add a splash of water.

Serve with warm pitta bread.

SERVES 2–4

#2
AVO ON TOAST

1 LARGE EGG
1 RIPE AVOCADO, PEELED, STONED AND
  SLICED
1 TBSP OLIVE OIL
1 TBSP LEMON JUICE
1 SLICE OF SOURDOUGH BREAD, TOASTED
1 BIRD'S-EYE (THAI) CHILLI, FINELY
  CHOPPED
1 RADISH, SLICED
SALT AND FRESHLY GROUND BLACK PEPPER

Boil the egg in a pan of boiling water for 5 minutes so the yolk remains soft.

Meanwhile, toss the sliced avocado with the olive oil and lemon juice. Spread the avocado mixture onto the toast, squashing it down with the knife. Scatter on the chopped chilli and sliced radish.

Peel the egg and place it on top of the avocado toast. Finish with a good grind of salt and pepper.

**SERVES
1**

#3
EGGS BENEDICT

125 G/4½ OZ/½ CUP BUTTER
2 EGG YOLKS
½ TSP DIJON MUSTARD
1 TBSP LEMON JUICE
½ TSP WHITE WINE VINEGAR
½ TBSP OLIVE OIL
100 G/3½ OZ BABY SPINACH
SALT AND FRESHLY GROUND BLACK PEPPER
1 SLICE OF GOOD PARMA HAM
  (PROSCIUTTO)
2 EGGS
1 ENGLISH MUFFIN

**SERVES
1**

Preheat the grill.

To make the hollandaise, melt the butter in a small pan. Put the egg yolks into a heatproof bowl set over a pan of gently simmering water and whisk with the mustard and a squeeze of lemon juice until thick. Remove from the heat and slowly whisk in the melted butter until the mixture is creamy. Loosen with a splash of water if needed. Whisk in the vinegar and keep the sauce warm over the pan of hot water.

Heat the oil in a large pan, add the spinach and cook until wilted. Transfer to a colander and squeeze out any excess water. Season and set aside.

Cook the Parma ham under the hot grill until crisp.

Poach the eggs in a pan of boiling salted water for about 3 minutes so that the yolk remains runny.

To serve, halve and toast the muffin, then top each half with spinach, shards of crispy ham and a poached egg. Pour over the hollandaise sauce and serve immediately.

#4
FRITTATA

1 TBSP BUTTER
1 SMALL ONION, SLICED
4 ASPARAGUS STALKS, ROUGHLY CHOPPED
6 EGGS
SALT AND FRESHLY GROUND BLACK PEPPER
100 G/3½ OZ/1 CUP BLUE CHEESE,
  CRUMBLED
HANDFUL OF BASIL LEAVES, CHOPPED

Preheat the grill to high.

Melt the butter in a non-stick, ovenproof pan over a medium heat, add the onion and fry for 4 minutes. Add the asparagus and sauté for 3 minutes.

Whisk the eggs in a separate bowl and season well with salt and pepper. Add the eggs to the pan and stir to distribute evenly. Cook gently on the hob for 4 minutes, or until the mixture begins to set around the edges.

Sprinkle over the blue cheese and place the pan under the grill for 2–3 minutes until golden and bubbly. Scatter with basil leaves, slice and serve from the pan.

SERVES
4

#5
BLUEBERRY MUFFINS

40 G/5 OZ/¾ CUP CASTER (SUPERFINE)
  SUGAR
1 LARGE EGG
115 ML/4 FL OZ/½ CUP VEGETABLE OIL
75 ML/2½ FL OZ/⅓ CUP MILK
1 TSP VANILLA EXTRACT
225 G/8 OZ/1¾ CUPS SELF-RAISING (SELF-
  RISING) FLOUR
1 TSP BAKING POWDER
¼ TSP SALT
75 ML/2½ FL OZ/⅓ CUP PLAIN YOGURT
1 SMALL PUNNET/1 PINT OF BLUEBERRIES
1 TBSP CASTER (SUPERFINE) SUGAR, FOR
  SPRINKLING

Preheat the oven to 200°C/400°F/Gas mark 6. Line a muffin tin with 8–12 muffin cases, according to how big you want to make them.

Combine the sugar, egg, oil, milk and vanilla in a large bowl and stir well.

Sift the flour, baking powder and salt into another bowl, then stir them into the wet ingredients until combined. Don't over-mix – just stir until there are no lumps. Mix in the yogurt until it is well distributed. Fold in the blueberries, saving a few for the muffin tops.

Spoon the batter into the muffin cases. Add the remaining blueberries to the top and sprinkle with sugar. Bake in the oven for 25 minutes, or until golden brown.

MAKES 8–12 MUFFINS

#6
CIABATTA PIZZA

1 SMALL CIABATTA LOAF, SLICED IN HALF
2 TBSP TOMATO PURÉE (PASTE)
2 TBSP OLIVE OIL, PLUS EXTRA FOR
   DRIZZLING
2 GARLIC CLOVES, CRUSHED
SALT AND FRESHLY GROUND BLACK PEPPER
1 MUSHROOM, SLICED
PITTED BLACK OLIVES, SLICED
3 CHERRY TOMATOES, SLICED IN HALF
2 BASIL LEAVES
150 G/5½ OZ FRESH MOZZARELLA, TORN
SMALL HANDFUL OF ROCKET (ARUGULA)
   LEAVES

Preheat the grill to medium.

Grill the ciabatta slices, cut side up, under the grill until slightly golden.

Mix the tomato purée, olive oil, garlic and salt and pepper together in a bowl.

Spread the tomato paste up to the edges of the bread. Top with the mushrooms, olives, tomatoes, basil and mozzarella, or use any of your favourite toppings! Add a grind of pepper and drizzle with olive oil.

Grill for 10 minutes, or until the cheese is golden and bubbly. Scatter with rocket leaves and serve.

SERVES 2

#7
CHEESEBURGER

500 G/1LB 2OZ/2¼ CUPS MINCED (GROUND)
  BEEF
1 SMALL RED ONION, FINELY SLICED
1 SMALL GARLIC CLOVE, CRUSHED
1 EGG
SALT AND FRESHLY GROUND BLACK PEPPER
VEGETABLE OIL, FOR BRUSHING
4 BURGER BUNS, HALVED

TO SERVE
KETCHUP
CHILLI SAUCE
MUSTARD
BLUE CHEESE
ICEBERG LETTUCE
TOMATOES, SLICED

Put the beef, onion, garlic and egg in a bowl. Season well with salt and pepper and mix together. Divide the mixture into four portions and shape into patties. Leave them to firm up in the fridge for 30 minutes.

Heat a barbecue or griddle pan.

Brush the burgers with oil and cook on the barbecue or hot griddle for 4–6 minutes on each side, depending on how you like them.

Heat the halved burger buns, cut side down, for 1 minute on the barbecue or griddle pan. Pop a burger inside each bun and finish with your favourite toppings. Try ketchup, chilli sauce, mustard or blue cheese with lettuce and sliced tomato.

**SERVES
4**

#8
MAC 'N' CHEESE

300 G/10½ OZ MACARONI OR SHORT PASTA
A LITTLE OIL, FOR COOKING PASTA
2 TBSP BUTTER
1 GARLIC CLOVE, CRUSHED
1 TSP ENGLISH MUSTARD POWDER
2½ TBSP PLAIN (ALL-PURPOSE) FLOUR
500 ML/18 FL OZ/2 CUPS WHOLE MILK
200 G/7 OZ/2¼ CUPS MATURE CHEDDAR
  CHEESE, GRATED
200 G/7 OZ PROCESSED CHEESE SLICES
SALT AND FRESHLY GROUND BLACK PEPPER
½ TSP PAPRIKA

Preheat the oven to 200°C/400°F/Gas mark 6.

Cook the macaroni in a pan of boiling water for 8–10 minutes, or until al dente. Drain and return to the pan with a little oil to stop it sticking.

Melt the butter in a saucepan over a medium heat, add the garlic and mustard powder and cook for 1 minute, then stir in the flour. Cook for a further minute, then gradually whisk in the milk and simmer for 5 minutes, whisking constantly until thickened.

Remove the pan from the heat, add the cheeses and stir until the cheese melts. Season with salt and pepper.

Pour the cheesy sauce over the pasta and mix gently until the pasta is coated. Tip the mixture into a large ovenproof dish. Sprinkle with paprika and bake in the oven for 20 minutes, or until golden and bubbly.

**SERVES
4**

#9
CHILLI

1 TBSP OLIVE OIL
1 LARGE ONION, FINELY CHOPPED
1 CELERY STICK, FINELY CHOPPED
3 GARLIC CLOVES, CRUSHED
1 TSP HOT CHILLI POWDER
1 TSP GROUND CUMIN
1 TSP PAPRIKA
½ TSP GROUND CINNAMON
1 TSP DRIED OREGANO
1 GREEN (BELL) PEPPER, CHOPPED
500 G/1 LB 2OZ/2¼ CUPS LEAN MINCED
  (GROUND) BEEF
1 TBSP TOMATO PURÉE
400 G/14 OZ CAN CHOPPED TOMATOES
1 BEEF STOCK CUBE
SALT AND FRESHLY GROUND BLACK PEPPER
400 G/14 OZ CAN RED KIDNEY BEANS,
  DRAINED AND RINSED
COOKED BASMATI RICE, TO SERVE

Heat the oil in a large saucepan over a medium heat, add the onion and celery and fry for about 5 minutes. Add the garlic, spices, oregano and green pepper and fry for a further 5 minutes.

Increase the heat and gradually add the mince, breaking it up with a wooden spoon. Stir until well browned. Add the tomato pureé, canned tomatoes and half a can of water. Crumble in the stock cube, season with salt and pepper and stir well. Cover and simmer for 30 minutes, stirring occasionally. Add the drained beans and cook for a further 10 minutes.

Serve with basmati rice.

**SERVES
4**

#10
THAI GREEN CURRY

100 G/3½ OZ FINE
  GREEN BEANS, TRIMMED AND HALVED
1 TBSP VEGETABLE OR SUNFLOWER OIL
1 GARLIC CLOVE, CHOPPED
4 TSP THAI GREEN CURRY PASTE
400 ML/14 FL OZ CAN COCONUT MILK
2 KAFFIR LIME LEAVES, FINELY SHREDDED
1 TSP BROWN SUGAR
450 G/1 LB SKINLESS CHICKEN BREASTS,
  DICED
2 TSP THAI FISH SAUCE
SALT AND FRESHLY GROUND BLACK PEPPER
(OPTIONAL)
HANDFUL OF BASIL LEAVES
COOKED THAI JASMINE RICE, TO SERVE

Steam the green beans for 3 minutes, then refresh under cold water and set aside.

Heat the oil in a wok over a high heat until smoking. Drop in the garlic and cook for a few seconds. Add the curry paste and stir-fry for 1–2 minutes to release the flavours. Add the coconut milk, lime leaves and sugar and stir well. Bring the mixture to the boil, then reduce the heat until the mixture is simmering. Add the chicken, cover and simmer for 8 minutes, or until the chicken is cooked.

Add the fish sauce, then taste and season with salt and pepper, if needed. Tip in the reserved green beans and warm them through.

Scatter basil leaves over the curry and serve with jasmine rice.

**SERVES
4-6**

#11
LASAGNE

1 TBSP OLIVE OIL
1 LARGE ONION, FINELY CHOPPED
1 LARGE GARLIC CLOVE, CRUSHED
500 G/1 LB 2OZ/2¼ CUPS LEAN MINCED
  (GROUND) BEEF
2–3 TBSP TOMATO PURÉE (PASTE)
600 G/1 LB 5OZ CANNED CHOPPED
  TOMATOES
2 TSP MIXED DRIED HERBS
1 TBSP BROWN SUGAR
SALT AND FRESHLY GROUND BLACK PEPPER
200 G/7 OZ QUICK-COOK LASAGNE
2 BALLS OF MOZZARELLA, SLICED
75 G/2¾ OZ/1 CUP PARMESAN CHEESE,
  GRATED

Preheat the oven to 200°C/400°F/Gas mark 6. Grease a
large ovenproof dish.

Heat the oil in a large pan, add the onion and garlic and
fry until soft. Add the mince and fry, breaking it up with a
wooden spoon until brown. Add the tomato pureé and fry
for a further 2 minutes, then tip in the canned tomatoes,
herbs and sugar. Season with salt and pepper, stir well and
simmer for 20 minutes, or until the sauce becomes thick.

Spoon enough of the sauce into the prepared dish to
cover the base, then arrange a single layer of lasagne
sheets on top. Continue to layer up the sauce and lasagne
until you have three layers. Arrange the mozzarella slices
on top of the lasagne and sprinkle over the Parmesan.

Bake in the oven for 30–40 minutes until bubbling
and golden.

**SERVES
4**

#12
AUBERGINE PARMIGIANA

3 TBSP OLIVE OIL
1 GARLIC CLOVE, CRUSHED
1 TSP DRIED OREGANO
1 ONION, CHOPPED
2 X 400 G/14 OZ CANNED CHOPPED
   TOMATOES
½ TSP CHILLI (RED PEPPER) FLAKES
HANDFUL OF BASIL LEAVES, ROUGHLY
   CHOPPED
SALT AND FRESHLY GROUND BLACK PEPPER
2 EGGS
2 TBSP WATER
130 G/4¾ OZ/1⅔ CUPS BREADCRUMBS
2 AUBERGINES (EGGPLANTS), CUT INTO
   1 CM/½ IN THICK SLICES
100 G/3½ OZ/1½ CUPS GRATED PARMESAN
1 BALL OF MOZZARELLA, TORN

**SERVES
4-6**

Preheat the oven to 190°C/375°F/Gas mark 5. Grease a large ovenproof dish.

Heat 1 tablespoon of oil in a large pan over a medium heat, add the garlic, oregano and onion and fry until soft, then add the tomatoes and chilli flakes and stir well. Lower the heat and simmer for about 15–20 minutes until the sauce has reduced slightly. Remove the pan from the heat, add the chopped basil and season with salt and pepper.

Meanwhile, beat the eggs and water together in a bowl, then pour the breadcrumbs onto a plate. Dip each slice of aubergine into the beaten eggs, and then into the breadcrumbs, making sure to coat them all over.

Heat the remaining oil in a large frying pan over a high heat, then add the aubergine slices, reduce the heat to medium and fry on both sides until golden and soft, about 3 minutes. You may need to do this in batches.

Spread a layer of sauce over the base of the prepared dish. Cover with slices of aubergine, then sprinkle with Parmesan. Repeat the layers until all the ingredients are used up, finishing with a layer of sauce. Top with the torn mozzarella.

Bake in the oven for 30 minutes, or until crisp and bubbling.

#13
CHICKEN NOODLE SOUP

2 TBSP OLIVE OIL
1 GARLIC CLOVE, CRUSHED
1 MEDIUM ONION, CHOPPED
2 MEDIUM CARROTS, PEELED AND CHOPPED
1 CELERY STICK, FINELY CHOPPED
1 BAY LEAF
SALT AND FRESHLY GROUND BLACK PEPPER
1.5 LITRES/2½ PINTS/6⅓ CUPS CHICKEN
   STOCK (BROTH)
500 G/1 LB 2OZ SKINLESS CHICKEN BREAST,
   DICED
125 G/4½ OZ DRIED SPAGHETTI
2 TSP CHOPPED THYME

Heat the oil in a large saucepan over a medium heat, add
the garlic and all the chopped vegetables, season with a
little salt and pepper and fry for 2–3 minutes. Add the bay
leaf and pour in the stock. Bring to the boil, then add the
chicken. Return to the boil, reduce the heat and simmer
for 3 minutes.

Add the spaghetti and cook for about 6–7 minutes, or until
the pasta is al dente. Remove the pan from the heat once
the pasta and chicken are cooked. Stir in the thyme leaves,
remove the bay leaf and serve piping hot.

**SERVES
4-6**

#14
CORN CHOWDER

1 TBSP OLIVE OIL
1 MEDIUM ONION, FINELY CHOPPED
1 RED (BELL) PEPPER, DESEEDED AND
  CHOPPED
1 CELERY STICK, FINELY CHOPPED
1 GARLIC CLOVE, CRUSHED
1 MEDIUM POTATO, CUBED
1 TBSP PLAIN (ALL-PURPOSE) FLOUR
700ML/1¼ PINTS/3 CUPS SEMI-SKIMMED
  MILK
200 ML/7 FL OZ/SCANT 1 CUP VEGETABLE
  STOCK
325 G/11½ OZ CAN SWEETCORN, DRAINED
  AND RINSED
SALT AND FRESHLY GROUND BLACK PEPPER
2 TBSP CHOPPED CHIVES

Heat the oil in a large saucepan over a medium heat, add
the onion, pepper, celery and garlic and fry for 5 minutes
until the vegetables have softened. Add the potato and
sprinkle over the flour. Stir for a few minutes.

Pour in the milk and vegetable stock and bring to the boil.
Reduce the heat and simmer, stirring frequently, for about
10 minutes, or until the potato is tender.

Tip in the sweetcorn and warm through. Season with salt
and pepper and serve topped with chives.

**SERVES
4**

#15
PESTO GRILLED CHEESE SANDWICH

1 TBSP SOFTENED BUTTER
2 THICK SLICES OF BREAD
1 HEAPED TSP GREEN PESTO
1 TBSP CREAM CHEESE
110 G/4 OZ/1¼ CUPS CHEDDAR CHEESE,
  GRATED
1 TOMATO, SLICED

Heat a frying pan over a medium heat. Butter a slice of
bread and place it buttered side down in the pan.

Now spread half of the pesto over the exposed side of
the bread in the pan. Top with the cream cheese, grated
Cheddar and slices of tomato.

Spread the remaining pesto on the second slice of bread
and place it on top of the sandwich, pesto side down.
Butter the top of the sandwich and fry until both sides are
golden and the cheese has melted.

**SERVES
1**

#16
CAULIFLOWER AND BROCCOLI BAKE

1 CAULIFLOWER, IN FLORETS
1 SMALL HEAD OF BROCCOLI, IN FLORETS
2 TBSP BUTTER
2 TBSP PLAIN (ALL-PURPOSE) FLOUR
1 TSP ENGLISH MUSTARD POWDER
500 ML/18 FL OZ/2 CUPS SEMI-SKIMMED MILK
150 G/5½ OZ/1⅔ CUPS MATURE (SHARP) CHEDDAR CHEESE, GRATED
SALT AND FRESHLY GROUND BLACK PEPPER
2 SPRING ONIONS (SCALLIONS), CHOPPED
½ TSP PAPRIKA

Preheat the oven to 180°C/350°F/Gas mark 4.

Boil the cauliflower in a large pan for 5 minutes, then add the broccoli and cook for a further 3 minutes. Drain and spread the vegetables out in a large ovenproof dish.

For the sauce, melt the butter in a saucepan over a medium heat until beginning to bubble. Add the flour and mustard powder and whisk until smooth. Gradually pour in the milk, stirring constantly until the sauce thickens.

Remove the pan from the heat and stir in the cheese, reserving a handful for the top of the bake. Season with salt and pepper and add the spring onions.

Pour the sauce over the vegetables, then sprinkle with paprika and the reserved cheese. Bake in the oven for 35–40 minutes until golden and bubbling.

SERVES 6

#17
STEAK AND CHIPS

1 TBSP LEMON JUICE
2 TBSP WHITE WINE VINEGAR
PINCH OF ENGLISH MUSTARD POWDER
1 SHALLOT, FINELY CHOPPED
1 TSP BLACK PEPPERCORNS
2 EGG YOLKS, BEATEN
150 G/5½ OZ/⅔ CUP BUTTER, MELTED
SALT AND FRESHLY GROUND BLACK PEPPER
2 TBSP FRESH TARRAGON, CHOPPED
150 G/5½ OZ WHITE POTATOES, CUT INTO
   BATONS
VEGETABLE OIL, FOR DEEP-FRYING AND
   BRUSHING
200 G/7 OZ RUMP (SIRLOIN) STEAK

**SERVES
1**

For the béarnaise sauce, place the lemon juice, white wine, mustard powder, shallot and peppercorns in a small saucepan and bring to the boil. Lower the heat and simmer until the liquid has reduced by half, then strain into a medium heatproof bowl.

Place the heatproof bowl over a pan of simmering water, making sure that the base of the bowl does not touch the water. Pour in the beaten egg yolks and whisk until pale and frothy. Gradually add the melted butter, whisking constantly to make a thick, creamy sauce. Season with salt and pepper and stir in the chopped tarragon. Turn off the heat and leave the bowl over the pan until ready to serve.

Rinse the potato batons and pat dry on a clean tea towel. Place them in a deep saucepan and just cover with cold oil. Bring the oil to a simmer over a medium heat and give the chips a stir. Increase the heat so the oil is bubbling and fry the chips, stirring occasionally for 15 minutes, or until golden and crisp. Remove the cooked chips and drain on kitchen paper, then set aside.

Heat a griddle pan until smoking hot. Season the steak with salt and pepper and brush with a little oil. Cook the steak for 2 minutes on each side, then leave to rest on a plate.

To serve, spoon the béarnaise sauce over the steak and serve with a stack of chips on the side.

#18
FRENCH ONION SOUP

50 G/1¾ OZ/2 TBSP BUTTER
6 LARGE WHITE ONIONS, SLICED
2 THYME SPRIGS
1 BAY LEAF
3 GARLIC CLOVES, FINELY SLICED
2 TBSP PLAIN (ALL-PURPOSE) FLOUR
1.5 LITRES/2½ PINTS/6⅓ CUPS HOT BEEF
   STOCK (BROTH)
1 LARGE GLASS OF WHITE WINE
SALT AND FRESHLY GROUND BLACK PEPPER
1 BAGUETTE, THINLY SLICED
200 G/7 OZ/1¾ CUPS GRUYÈRE CHEESE,
   GRATED

Melt the butter in a large heavy-based pan over a low heat, add the onions, thyme sprigs and bay leaf and fry gently for 30 minutes, stirring frequently until the onions are soft and caramelized, but not burnt. Add the garlic and fry for a further 5 minutes. Discard the bay leaf and thyme.

Stir in the flour and cook for 3–4 minutes. Increase the heat and pour in the hot beef stock and the wine. Partially cover with a lid and simmer for 30 minutes. Season well with salt and pepper.

Preheat the grill to medium and lightly toast the bread on one side. Turn the bread over, pile on the grated cheese and grill until melted.

Ladle the soup into warm bowls and place 1–2 slices of cheesy toast on top.

**SERVES
4–6**

#19
TUNA MELT

200 G/7 OZ CAN SUSTAINABLE TUNA,
  DRAINED
2 SMALL SPRING ONIONS (SCALLIONS),
  SLICED
SMALL HANDFUL OF BASIL, CHOPPED
4 TBSP MAYONNAISE
SALT AND FRESHLY GROUND BLACK PEPPER
2 SLICES SOURDOUGH BREAD
60 G/2¼ OZ/⅔ CUP CHEDDAR CHEESE,
  GRATED
½ TSP PAPRIKA

Preheat the grill to high.

Mix the tuna in a bowl with the spring onions, chopped basil and mayonnaise. Season with salt and a good grind of black pepper.

Toast the bread under the grill on both sides, then spread the tuna mixture on top. Scatter over the cheese and return to the grill until bubbling.

Sprinkle over the paprika, slice and serve.

**SERVES
1**

#20
FLAPJACKS

100 G/3½ OZ/7 TBSP UNSALTED BUTTER
100 G/3½ OZ/⅓ CUP GOLDEN (LIGHT CORN)
  SYRUP
100 G/3½ OZ/½ CUP LIGHT MUSCOVADO
  (BROWN) SUGAR
225 G/8 OZ/2⅔ CUPS PORRIDGE (ROLLED)
  OATS
50 G/1¾ OZ/¼ CUP DRIED APRICOTS,
  CHOPPED
50 G/1¾ OZ/⅓ CUP DRIED CHERRIES

Preheat the oven to 180°C/350°F/Gas mark 4. Line a
23cm/9in square baking tin with parchment paper.

Melt the butter, syrup and sugar in a large saucepan over a
low heat. Stir in the oats, making sure they are thoroughly
coated in the syrup. Mix in the dried apricots and cherries.

Pour the mixture into the prepared tin and press it flat
with the back of a spoon. Bake in the oven for 20–25
minutes, depending on whether you like your flapjacks
chewy or crunchy.

Remove from the oven and cut into slices while still hot.
Allow the flapjacks to cool before removing from the tin.

**MAKES
12
SLICES**

#21
PEANUT BUTTER COOKIES

110 G/4 OZ/1 STICK BUTTER, SOFTENED
100 G/3½ OZ/½ CUP GRANULATED SUGAR
85 G/3 OZ/7 TBSP LIGHT BROWN SUGAR
100 G/3½ OZ/SCANT ½ CUP CRUNCHY
  PEANUT BUTTER
1 TSP VANILLA EXTRACT
1 LARGE EGG
185 G/6 OZ/1⅓ CUPS PLAIN (ALL-PURPOSE)
  FLOUR
1 TSP BAKING POWDER
1 TSP BICARBONATE OF SODA (BAKING SODA)
1 TSP SALT
50 G/1¾ OZ/SCANT ⅓ CUP PLAIN
  (SEMISWEET) CHOCOLATE CHIPS

Preheat the oven to 180°C/350°F/Gas mark 4. Line a baking sheet with parchment paper.

Beat the butter and sugars in a mixer on medium speed for about 3 minutes, or until light and fluffy. Beat in the peanut butter until smooth, then the vanilla extract, then the egg.

Combine the flour, baking powder, bicarbonate of soda and salt in a bowl. Set the mixer on a slow speed and gradually add the dry ingredients until it is a smooth dough. Finally, fold in the chocolate chips.

Form the dough into balls (about 1 heaped tablespoon per ball), and place on the prepared baking sheet about 8cm/3in apart. Flatten each ball with the back of a fork.

Bake for 10–12 minutes, or until the edges are golden and the centres are slightly puffy. Cool on a wire rack.

MAKES 12 COOKIES

#22
BAKED CAMEMBERT

1 BOXED CAMEMBERT
1 GARLIC CLOVE, THINLY SLICED
FRESH ROSEMARY TIPS
OLIVE OIL, FOR DRIZZLING

TO SERVE
2 TBSP WALNUTS, CHOPPED
2 TBSP DRIED CRANBERRIES, CHOPPED
1 BAGUETTE

Preheat the oven to 200°C/400°F/Gas mark 6.

Remove any plastic packaging from the cheese and return it to its box, leaving the lid off.

Pierce the top of the cheese with a sharp knife and insert slices of garlic and rosemary tips into the slits.

Drizzle with oil and place the boxed cheese on a baking sheet. Bake in the oven for 10 minutes, or until the centre of the cheese is melting.

To serve, arrange the cheese, nuts, cranberries and bread on a large board. Scoop up some melted cheese with a chunk of bread and dip it into the chopped fruit and nuts.

SERVES 1–2

#23
TOAD IN THE HOLE

2 TBSP VEGETABLE OIL
8 HERBY PORK SAUSAGES
200 G/7 OZ/1½ CUPS PLAIN (ALL-PURPOSE)
  FLOUR
½ TSP ENGLISH MUSTARD POWDER
SALT AND FRESHLY GROUND BLACK PEPPER
3 EGGS
250 ML/9 FL OZ/GENEROUS 1 CUP SEMI-
  SKIMMED MILK
2 THYME SPRIGS, LEAVES PICKED

Preheat the oven to 200°C/400°F/Gas mark 6.

Pour the oil into the base of a large ovenproof dish. Toss the sausages in the oil and arrange them in a single layer. Bake in the oven for 10 minutes.

Meanwhile, mix the flour, mustard powder and a pinch of salt and pepper together in a medium bowl. Make a well in the centre of the flour and whisk in the eggs and half of the milk, gradually incorporating the flour from the edges. Whisk in the remaining milk to make a smooth batter. Stir in the thyme leaves.

Remove the sausages from the oven and quickly pour in the batter. The sausages should be three-quarters submerged. Return the dish to the oven and bake for 35 minutes, or until the centre is risen and golden and the batter is set.

**SERVES
4-6**

#24
DAUPHINOISE POTATOES

8 LARGE WHITE POTATOES, PEELED
300 ML/10 FL OZ/1¼ CUPS DOUBLE (HEAVY)
  CREAM
300 ML/10 FL OZ/1¼ CUPS WHOLE MILK
PINCH OF GROUND NUTMEG
2 THYME SPRIGS
2 GARLIC CLOVES, PEELED
SALT AND FRESHLY GROUND BLACK PEPPER
50 G/1¾OZ/¾ CUP PARMESAN CHEESE,
  GRATED

Preheat the oven to 160°C/325°F/Gas mark 3. Grease a large ovenproof dish.

Finely slice the potatoes, about 3 mm/⅛ in thick. Put them in a bowl of water to keep them from turning brown.

Heat the cream, milk, nutmeg, thyme and whole garlic cloves in a saucepan. Bring to the boil, then reduce the heat and simmer for 2–3 minutes. Remove from the heat and allow to cool before straining the mixture into a jug.

Pat the potato slices dry on a clean tea towel and layer them in the prepared dish, overlapping the slices and seasoning each layer with salt and pepper. Pour over the garlic and thyme infused cream, making sure it seeps into all the gaps.

Bake in the oven for 50 minutes, or until the potatoes are soft. Increase the oven temperature to 180°C/350°F/Gas mark 4, scatter over the cheese and bake for a further 5–10 minutes until golden.

**SERVES
8**

#25
BANANA BREAD

90 G/3¼ OZ/SCANT ½ CUP UNSALTED
  BUTTER
110 G/4 OZ/½ CUP + 1 TBSP SOFT BROWN
  SUGAR
1 TSP VANILLA EXTRACT
5–6 OVERRIPE BANANAS, MASHED
2 EGGS, BEATEN
250 G/9 OZ/1¾ CUPS + 2 TBSP PLAIN
  (ALL-PURPOSE) FLOUR
1 TSP BICARBONATE OF SODA (BAKING
  SODA)
½ TSP GROUND CINNAMON
¼ TSP SALT
90 G/3¼ OZ MILK CHOCOLATE

Preheat the oven to 170°C/325°F/Gas mark 3. Grease and
line a 900 g/2 lb loaf tin.

Melt the butter, sugar and vanilla extract in a saucepan
over a medium heat. Remove from the heat and add the
mashed bananas and beaten eggs. Mix well.

Combine the flour, bicarbonate of soda, cinnamon and salt
in a separate bowl and stir in the banana mixture to make
a batter. Be careful not to overmix or the loaf will turn out
dry. Break the chocolate into small pieces and stir it into
the batter.

Pour into the prepared tin and bake in the centre of the
oven for 50 minutes, or until a skewer inserted into the
middle comes out clean. Allow to cool in the tin for 10
minutes, then turn out onto a wire rack.

**CUTS
INTO 12
SLICES**

#26
CARROT CAKE

500 G/1 LB 2OZ/2½ CUPS CASTER
  (SUPERFINE) SUGAR
400 G/14 OZ/3 CUPS PLAIN (ALL-PURPOSE)
  FLOUR
1 TSP SALT
2 TSP GROUND CINNAMON
1 TSP BAKING POWDER
1 TSP BICARBONATE OF SODA (BAKING SODA)
450 ML/16 FL OZ/2 CUPS VEGETABLE OIL
4 EGGS
450 G/1 LB CARROTS, PEELED AND GRATED
LARGE HANDFUL OF WALNUTS, CHOPPED

FOR THE FROSTING
400 G/14 OZ/1¾ CUPS CREAM CHEESE
110 G/4 OZ/1 STICK BUTTER
250 G/9 OZ/1¾ CUPS ICING
  (CONFECTIONERS') SUGAR
1 TSP VANILLA EXTRACT

Preheat the oven to 160°C/325°F/Gas mark 3. Grease and
line 2 x 23 cm/9 in cake tins with parchment paper.

Combine the sugar, flour, salt, cinnamon, baking powder,
bicarbonate of soda and oil in a large bowl. Beat in the
eggs one at a time, then stir in the carrots and walnuts.

Pour the batter into the cake tins and bake for 40 minutes,
or until a skewer inserted into the middle of the cakes
comes out clean. Leave the cakes to cool in their tins for
10 minutes, then turn onto a wire rack to cool.

Meanwhile, for the frosting, beat the cream cheese,
butter, icing sugar and vanilla extract together in a bowl
until fluffy. Spread on top of one cooled cake, put the
other cake on top and cover with the remaining frosting.

**CUTS
INTO 12
SLICES**

#27
PEANUT BUTTER BANANA FRENCH TOAST

1 EGG
½ TSP GROUND CINNAMON
¼ TSP VANILLA EXTRACT
2 TBSP SMOOTH PEANUT BUTTER
2 THICK SLICES WHITE BREAD
1 BANANA, SLICED
1 TBSP BUTTER
1 TSP ICING (CONFECTIONERS') SUGAR

Lightly beat the egg, cinnamon and vanilla extract together in a shallow dish.

Spread 1 tablespoon of peanut butter on each slice of bread. Place the banana slices on top of one of the slices of bread. Place the other slice of bread on top, peanut butter side down.

Melt the butter in a non-stick frying pan over a medium heat. Dip both sides of the sandwich into the egg mixture and place in the heated pan. Fry until golden on both sides. Sprinkle with icing sugar and serve warm.

**SERVES
1**

#28
APPLE AND BLACKBERRY CRUMBLE

4 EATING APPLES, PEELED AND CORED
2 TBSP CASTER (SUPERFINE) SUGAR
1 TSP GROUND CINNAMON
300 G/10½ OZ/2⅓ CUPS BLACKBERRIES

FOR THE TOPPING
170 G/6 OZ/1¼ CUPS PLAIN (ALL-PURPOSE)
   FLOUR
100 G/3½ OZ/½ CUP CASTER (SUPERFINE)
   SUGAR
100 G/3½ OZ/7 TBSP COLD, UNSALTED BUTTER
2 TBSP ROLLED OATS
1 TBSP DEMERARA (RAW BROWN) SUGAR

Preheat the oven to 190°C/375°F/Gas mark 5.

Slice the apples into 1 cm/½ in thick pieces and place in a large ovenproof dish. Sprinkle over half the sugar and cinnamon. Pour the blackberries on top and sprinkle over the remaining sugar and cinnamon. Make sure there are no large gaps for the topping to fall through.

To make the topping, put the flour and caster sugar in a bowl. Cut the butter into cubes, add to the mixture and rub into the flour until it resembles breadcrumbs. Pour the topping over the fruit in an even layer and press down gently. Sprinkle the oats and demerara sugar on top.

Set the dish on a baking tray and bake for 35–40 minutes, or until the top is golden and the apples are soft. Allow to cool for 10 minutes before serving.

**SERVES
4**

#29
GUACAMOLE AND NACHOS

2 RIPE MEDIUM AVOCADOS, PEELED AND
  STONED
1 SMALL RED ONION, FINELY CHOPPED
1 LIME
1 BUNCH OF CORIANDER (CILANTRO),
  CHOPPED
SALT AND FRESHLY GROUND BLACK PEPPER
5 TOMATOES, DICED
1 WHITE ONION, FINELY CHOPPED
4 GARLIC CLOVES, FINELY CHOPPED
175 G/6 OZ BAG TORTILLA CHIPS
1 435 G/16 OZ CAN REFRIED BEANS
1-2 JARRED JALEPEÑO CHILLIES, SLICED
300 G/10½ OZ/3⅓ CUPS CHEDDAR CHEESE,
  GRATED

Preheat the oven to 200°C/400°F/Gas mark 6.

For the guacamole, scoop the avocado flesh into a bowl and mash with a fork. Stir in the red onion, a squeeze of lime juice and a handful of the chopped coriander. Season with salt and pepper, then cover and chill until needed.

To make the salsa, combine the diced tomatoes, white onion, garlic and remaining coriander in a bowl. Add a pinch of salt and pepper and the juice of ½ lime. Mix well, then cover and chill.

Spread the tortilla chips over the base of a large ovenproof dish. Spoon refried beans over the top, then scatter with sliced jalapeños. Top with grated cheese and bake for 15 minutes, or until the cheese has melted. Serve with the salsa and guacamole on the side.

**SERVES
4**

#30
KEY LIME PIE

125 G/4½ OZ/½ CUP UNSALTED BUTTER
300 G/10½ OZ GINGERNUT BISCUITS
  (COOKIES), CRUSHED
3 EGG YOLKS
400 G/14 OZ CAN CONDENSED MILK
GRATED ZEST AND JUICE OF 4 LIMES, PLUS
  EXTRA GRATED LIME ZEST TO SERVE
300 ML/10 FL OZ/1¼ CUPS DOUBLE (HEAVY)
  CREAM
1 TBSP ICING (CONFECTIONERS') SUGAR

Preheat the oven to 170°C/325°F/Gas mark 3.

Melt the butter in a pan. Turn off the heat and stir in the
crushed biscuits until completely coated. Press the mixture
into the base and sides of a 23 cm/9 in circular loose-
based tart tin. Bake in the oven for 10 minutes, then remove
from the oven and allow to cool. Keep the oven on.

Put the egg yolks in a large bowl and whisk for 1 minute.
Pour in the condensed milk and whisk for a further 3
minutes. Add the lime juice and zest and whisk again for
a few minutes. Pour the filling into the cooled base then
return it to the oven for 15 minutes. Allow to cool, then
transfer the pie to the fridge and chill for at least 3 hours.

To serve, remove the pie from the tin and place on a
serving plate. Softly whip the cream and icing sugar
together. Dollop the cream on top of the pie and finish
with a sprinkle of lime zest.

CUTS
INTO
8–10
SLICES

#31
GARLIC BREAD WITH MOZZARELLA

1 BAGUETTE
100 G/3½ OZ/7 TBSP SALTED BUTTER,
  SOFTENED
4 GARLIC CLOVES, CRUSHED
SMALL BUNCH OF PARSLEY, CHOPPED
1 BALL OF MOZZARELLA, SLICED

Preheat the oven to 180°C/350°F/Gas mark 4.

Make 2.5 cm/1 in thick slices all along the baguette, without cutting through the bottom crust.

Place the softened butter in a small bowl, add the garlic and parsley and mix together. Spread the butter mixture between the slices, then push a piece of mozzarella between each slice.

Wrap the bread in foil and bake in the oven for 15 minutes, or until the bread is crisp and the mozzarella is oozing.

**SERVES
6**

#32
CHEESY CORN ON THE COB

2 TBSP MAYONNAISE
SEA SALT
½ TSP CAYENNE PEPPER
1 LIME
2 CORN ON THE COBS
60 G/2¼ OZ/½ CUP FETA CHEESE,
  CRUMBLED
LIME WEDGES, TO SERVE

Preheat the grill to high.

Whisk the mayonnaise, salt, cayenne pepper and a good squeeze of lime together in a bowl. Brush the corn on the cobs with the mayonnaise mixture. Put the crumbled feta on a plate and roll the cobs in the cheese.

Wrap each corn in foil and place under the grill for 10–15 minutes, turning occasionally, until the corn is cooked. Serve warm with lime wedges.

SERVES 2

#33
VEGETABLE QUESADILLAS

1 TBSP SUNFLOWER OIL
1 SMALL RED ONION
2 GARLIC CLOVES, CHOPPED
1 SMALL RED (BELL) PEPPER, CHOPPED
1 TSP CHILLI (RED PEPPER) FLAKES
½ TSP GROUND CUMIN
1 TSP SMOKED PAPRIKA
SALT AND FRESHLY GROUND BLACK PEPPER
4 LARGE FLOUR TORTILLAS
400 G/14 OZ CAN KIDNEY BEANS, DRAINED,
  RINSED AND MASHED
100 G/3½ OZ/1 CUP CHEDDAR CHEESE,
  GRATED
HANDFUL OF CORIANDER (CILANTRO),
  CHOPPED
SOUR CREAM, TO SERVE

Heat the oil in a large frying pan over a medium heat, add the onion, garlic and red pepper and fry for about 5 minutes, or until soft. Add the chilli flakes, cumin and smoked paprika and season well with salt and pepper. Sauté everything together for a few minutes.

Heat a griddle pan over a medium heat. Spread two tortillas with mashed beans. Spoon over the vegetable mixture, then sprinkle generously with grated cheese and a scattering of chopped coriander.

Top with the remaining tortillas to make two sandwiches. Cook on the griddle, one at a time, until the cheese melts. Flip the quesadilla and toast the other side until crisp and golden. Serve sliced into wedges, with sour cream.

**SERVES
4-6**

#34
ETON MESS

1 SMALL PUNNET/1 PINT OF STRAWBERRIES
450 ML/16 FL OZ/2 CUPS DOUBLE (HEAVY)
 CREAM
4 READY-MADE MERINGUES, CRUSHED
MINT SPRIGS, TO DECORATE

Purée half the strawberries in a blender. Keep four strawberries for the decoration and chop the remainder into quarters.

Whip the cream until it forms stiff peaks, then fold in the strawberry purée. Gently fold in the chopped strawberries and crushed meringue.

Spoon the Eton mess into glass dishes. Serve, decorated with a sprig of mint and a single strawberry.

SERVES 4

#35
HOUMOUS WITH PITTA BREAD

400 G/14 OZ CAN CHICKPEAS, DRAINED AND
  RINSED
JUICE OF 1 LEMON
2 GARLIC CLOVES
4 TBSP OLIVE OIL
3 TBSP TAHINI
1 TSP GROUND CUMIN
SALT
PAPRIKA, TO GARNISH
4 PITTA BREADS, TO SERVE

Blitz the chickpeas, lemon juice, garlic, oil, tahini, cumin and a good pinch of salt in a blender or food processor, to make a creamy purée. Add a splash of water to loosen the mixture if needed. Check the flavour and add more lemon, garlic or salt to taste.

Heap the houmous into a large bowl, sprinkle with paprika and serve with warm pitta bread.

**SERVES
2**

With thanks to Rebecca, Elena and Nic

First published in the United Kingdom in 2017 by
Pavilion
43 Great Ormond Street
London
WC1N 3HZ

ISBN 978-1-91104-247-1

A CIP catalogue record for this book is available from the British Library.

10 9 8 7 6 5 4 3 2 1

Reproduction by Rival Colour Ltd, UK
Printed and bound by 1010 Printing International Ltd, China
This book can be ordered direct from the publisher at www.pavilionbooks.com